Dedicated To:
My mom & dad
April 27, 1991

Written By: Abigail Gartland

Hello, my name is St. Valentine!

I was born in Italy in the 200s!

I loved Jesus very much from the time I was a little boy.

My love grew, and I even became a priest when I grew up.

During the time when I grew up, people were not allowed to say they loved Jesus.

For a while, I was on house arrest which means I had to stay at home all the time.

One day, while I was stuck in my house, a man brought his blind daughter to visit me.

He wanted his daughter to be healed, and asked if I could heal her with the power of God.

I prayed and asked Jesus to heal her.

There was a miracle, and the little girl could see! We were so happy!

My faith and love for Jesus continued through my whole life.

On February 14th, I went to Heaven to be with Jesus forever!

Do you want to be more like me?

You can celebrate my feast day with me on February 14th

This is also known as Valentine's day!

I am the patron saint of love!

I pray for you every day.

St. Valentine, Pray for us!

opyright:

ipart: © PentoolPixie © LimeandKiwiDesigns
censed purchased: 1/10/2024

About the Author

Abigail Gartland

I love the saints and I love my faith. The idea for sharing the stories of the saints with little ones came when my dear friends were expecting their first baby. I wanted to create something as unique and special as our friendship. Each book is dedicated to very special people and groups who have enriched my faith in different ways. I am blessed to write these stories and appreciate the unending support of my family and friends. When I am not writing, I am a middle school teacher. I hope you enjoy these stories. I pray for each and every person who opens one of my books to learn more about the saints.

Abbie

www.ingramcontent.com/pod-product-compliance
Lightning Source LLC
LaVergne TN
LVHW051043070526
838201LV00067B/4906